Usborne

Big Wipe-Clean Activity Book

Use the wipe-clean pens to doodle,
join the dots and find your way
through all the mazes in this book.

Illustrated by Stacey Lamb

Designed by Matt Durber and Claire Ever

Words by Jessica Greenwell

On the move

Join the dots to find out what all the animals are driving.

SCHOOL BUS

honk! honk!

Bu_s and flow rs

Doodle patterns on the bugs and flowers.

Pirate treasure

Help the pirate ship reach the treasure chest.

Hanging out clothes

Join the dots to finish the picture.

Tasty cakes

Help Mouse decorate
his freshly baked cakes.

Snowy forest

Help the bears find their way
home through the forest.

Under the sea

Join the dots to see what's under the sea.

Monsters and robots

Help Mouse make some more monsters from these blobs of paint.

Dog has turned this box into a robot. Can you doodle some more?

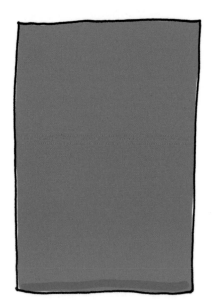

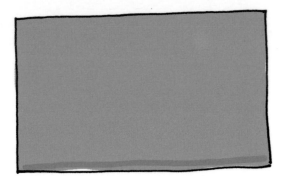

Out in space

Start at the big blue planet and find your way to Mouse's rocket.

How many blue stars can you count?

Join the dots to see what's at the building site.

In the street

Doodle smoke from
the chimneys.

Add windows and
doors to the houses.

Doodle clouds, rain and lightning in the sky.

In the town

The animals are driving home from town. Match each animal to its house and help them find their way back.

STORE

SCHOOL

Draw a star next to each bicycle. How many bicycles are there?

igh in the sky

Join the dots to see
what's up in the sky.

Wrapping presents

Doodle on the birthday presents and add ribbons, bows and tags.

Rescue the princess

Help Sir Mouse find two keys then rescue
Princess Hippo from the tower.

Beat the birds

Squirrel has found a tasty acorn. Which way should he go to avoid the hungry birds and get to the bottom of the tree?

How many red birds are there?

On the sea

Join the dots to finish this picture.

Fireworks fun